www.finishinglinepress.com

Letters to Littles' Mills

poems by

Mary Anna Dunn

Finishing Line Press
Georgetown, Kentucky

Letters to Littles' Mills

This collection is dedicated to all enslaved people.

ACKNOWLEDGMENTS

The italicized sections of the poems are quoted directly from letters written to
my ancestors at Littles' Mills. Most of the spirituals are from are from *Slaves
Songs of the United States* (Allen et al, 1867). Intertwined with these primary
sources are my own original writings, which though inspired by the letters,
are fictional. I have tried, in my poetry, to imagine the hidden lives of the
people barely referenced in the letters. I have no reason to believe that any of
the incidents narrated in the poetry ever occurred at Littles' Mills, although
they do reflect what I've heard and read about the lives of enslaved people
throughout The South. More information about the development of the
poems, including scans of the letters that inspired them, is available at www.
maryannadunnpoetand.

Thanks to Jessica Ney-Grimm for her assistance with fonts. Thanks to the
Richmond County Historical Society, the North Carolina Department of
Natural and Cultural Resources, and Blake McDonald for their help with
questions that came up about the John and Frances Little Home Place.

Publisher: Leah Maines
Editor: Christen Kincaid
Cover Art: "Littles' Mills" by Elizabeth Clarke. New York Public Library,
Digital Collections, Public Domain: Branding Slaves, Blake, William O.
Twenty-eight fugitives escaping from the Eastern Shore of Maryland. Still,
William. Unloading the rice-barges. King, Edwards.
Author Photo: Anna Lijing Dunn
Cover Design: Elizabeth Maines McCleavy

Printed in the USA on acid-free paper.
Order online: www.finishinglinepress.com
also available on amazon.com

Author inquiries and mail orders:
Finishing Line Press
P. O. Box 1626
Georgetown, Kentucky 40324
U. S. A.

Table of Contents

1799 -1825

Letters to Billy Little from his brothers and nephew in North West England and his son in New England.

The Reaping

Horizon wide that amber
　　　scythe harvest
bent double calico
　　　sun scorched ghosts my life
you reap

Sir,
I have never had the fortune to fall
into any satuation but as
a Servant in husbandry. England
at the present time, as I have no doubt
you have been informed, is in distressed
satuation and all most every
class of people and trades are laboring
under verry trying circumstances.

> If I don't see you more,
> Now God bless you, now God bless you,
> If I don't see you more.

A great number of laborers are not
employed and those that have employment their
wages are so small they cannot maintain
their families, but what is still more to be
lamented is many cannot be hired at all.
Such is my satuation at present
which induces me to write you as friend
and countryman. Your petitioner is
fully persuaded you will do everything
in your power to assist me in Bread
providing it is advisable for me
to come to America. Yours, Joseph

You are the bread that I eat still
　　　I am the grains you sowed and milled

hands and water
    turn the wheel
and grind the bread that I eat still.

Dear Brothers,
I take the pleasure of writing you
a few lins in Joseph's Leter as he
wishes to com to America if
                We part in the body but we meet in the spirit.
you think you could get him a situation,
we wish you to indevour. I think you
could get him work as an overseer
in such a place as Brother Thomas had.

            Good-bye my brother, good-bye. Hallelujah!

The Little Brothers Stock Their Farms

I understand Thomas has ben traverlen
a good while last year purchesen negers
in the north country and made som good

> Turn, sinner, turn today, Turn sinner, turn O!
> Tomorrow's sun will sure to shine, Turn sinner, turn O.

purchases and he speks of going to
soom other part to puches some Land I
wish it may be for all your goods

> Oh sinner, you make mistake, Turn sinner, turn O

and you wish to becom a fermer ferming
is a poor busness in this Countery
at this time everything is got quite low
in this part since peace takes place nothing sells
so well as wool I am wintering

> The sun may shine, but on your grave, Turn sinner,

about twelve hundred sheep this year

Exchange of Goods

1

The ocean is the same on every shore.
                    Heaving greys and greens release the scent
of brine and kelp onto the seething air

just the same in Liverpool and Lisbon
                    as in Senegambia and Newport.
Harbors change, but the ocean is the same.

2

Cowrie shells come from the ocean. Wool comes
                    from England: woolen cloth protects against
the Gulf of Guinea's chilling wind.

Twenty cabess of cowries, ten wool cloths,
                    two hundred pounds of gunpowder, or forty
iron bars. This is the value of a man.

3

When Haso first heard the raiders coming, he
                    gathered up cowrie shells. Enough of them might
buy freedom in America, or at least kindness.

4

On a slaver, no one can smell brine and kelp
                    above the death stench of captives
and sailors. Dying has been calculated

into every crossing. Haso, there are more of you
                    than needed on the far shore and more
of them than it will take to get you there.

5

But, Haso, you'll survive the middle passage and live
               to walk the long straight rows of strange landscapes.
You'll reach, sometimes, into the pocket of your stranger

clothes, fingertips touching small, smooth, glossy
               shells that knock together with a pleasing clink,
and have no more currency here than your name.

I Could Not Stay in Newark

I have left Newark on Christmas Day

    A baby born in Bethlehem and I heard from heaven today.
    A baby born in Bethlehem and I heard from heaven today.
    Hurry on my weary soul, And I heard from heaven today.

and went through New Haven, and got work
on Friday last but could not stay in Newark
for they work there harder than your negroes
                Hurry on my weary soul.

    Hurry on. Hurry on.

There is snow on the ground and the river
is froze across
            and you have left Newark on Christmas Day

I wish you would send me some papers so
I could read them.
They work there harder than your negroes.
I will stay in this part another winter.
I expect to come home in June
            The trumpet sound in the other bright land
            The trumpet sound in the other bright land
      Hurry on my weary soul, And I heard from heaven today.

For they work there harder than your negroes.
Here I make four dollars a month.
In Newark I got nothing.

          The bell is ringing in the other bright world
             Hurry on my weary soul.

The Lord in the Mists

All those fine rising sons of yours. I hope thay will
be all around your Table in hilth and the Lord in
the mists and that to Bles them when this come to
your hand—

1
On winter mornings ghosts
will escape the river.

2
Worn as a cloak by planter's sons
who steal through bedroom windows
                    towards the cringing cabins.

3
It clings like smoke to what
remains on the fields of Gettysburg.

4
Now the shrouded children
                    are walking to the kitchen.

5
So near that I can only dimly
see a woman
          standing next to me.

6
What has refused to be snow or rain
suffuses the air on Johnson's Island.

1847-1857

Letters to Fanny Myers Little from her friend in
New York City and from her parents,
Adeline and Absalom Myers, in Byhalia, Mississippi.

Aprons Are Very Fashionable

And now shall I tell you some particulars
respecting the fashions? They wear very small
bonnets indeed. Sacques are not worn
at all so I would not advise you
to make one of any kind.

I got a robe, you got a robe.

Very short flowing sleeves to everything
and large full undersleeves some with a wide
ruffle at the wrist, generally scalloped,
worked with large eyelet holes.

All of God's children got robes.

Aprons are very fashionable.
Small aprons of rich light colored silk
with shoulder straps of the same, narrow
at the waist and very wide so as to fall
from the shoulder.
Full lace aprons with colored ribbon run in the hem.

When I get to heaven I'm going to put on my robe.

All collars must lie down with the ribbons
above or under, not below, and the larger
the bow you can put in front the handsomer.
You remember my large red one. It is just right.
What a confused letter this must be. I have
told you the particulars of the fashions
but Fanny my head is not in them I hope.
The hand of Providence has led me.
How can I sufficiently praise him?

I'm going to shout all over heaven.

I have seen our dear Pastor and this evening
attended his weekly lecture—it was
on the text John 12.35
and very practical. Next Sunday
is our regular Communion season.
I hope, dear Fanny, that it may not be
long before you are permitted to enjoy
the feast of a Savior's love— think a great deal
about it and be not satisfied
until you have fulfilled the dying
command of your Savior.

      Everybody who's talking about heaven ain't going there.
French twists are out of fashion now. The latest
style is to part a great deal of hair forward
then comb the back hair up very high;
Puff the front as large as possible

      When I get to heaven, I'm going to put on my shoes.
Now dearest Fanny I hope you will
persevere in the faith of duty which
you will ever find pleasant. Study your Bible
and pray much.

      I'm going to walk all over heaven.
      Heaven. Heaven. Heaven.

The Wedding Gift

1

The quilt she knows she'll never make
Emmy keeps as scraps in a closed box
            on the floor of her one small room.
Butter-white homespun cotton, jean
            from Brother Sam's winter pants,
Sunday Meeting best brocade
            given to her mother
by the old mistress when it tore,
            and pieces of Sister's
linsey-woolsey baby clothes.

2

At the age of twelve,
            Emmy was brought to Littles' Mills
with Miss Fanny and her husband.
            She was a wedding present
from the bride's parents.
            On the train to Carolina
Emmy held a bag of rags to her chest
            like a nursling child. As she slept,
the whispered love-talk of her new owners
            faded like smoke that trailed behind them
all the way back to Oxford.
            As the train pulled into Charlotte, Emmy
thought she heard her mother calling,
            but it was only Miss Fanny shaking her awake.

3

Mornings, a squalid light passes
over her splintered windowsill
            and briefly catches on a line of those strange
white shells Emmy finds sometimes in the garden
            and collects like coins.
A quilt could make her corn shuck mattress warmer,
            brighten the dreary of her attic room,
but some things once closed cannot again be opened.

Cry Holy

I have rented for next year the field
on toward the Stream Mill. I get $890
reserving a field at the same rate worth
about $60.

    Absalom stands with a neighbor
        by the mill stream discussing plans to lease his land.
    Upstream, his maid's two daughters fill buckets
        for the washing. The youngest pauses, picks up a stick
    and tosses it onto the rushing current.
        For one small moment, four pairs of eyes
    are transfixed by the stick, laughing past them
        on the water's cool and roil until it cannot be seen.
    Polly's daughters again take up their pails,
        and the two old men shake hands to close the deal.

The bad weather lately and the lateness
of the cotton in opening will
shorten it from what I ought to have made.

    Back at the big house, finished with her washing,
        their mother pitches the water up into the air
    where it fractures and hangs on the morning sun.
                    Every hour in the day, cry holy,
                        Cry holy, my lord
                    Every hour in the day, cry holy
                    Oh show me the crime I've done.

It Must Have Been the Muscadines

While Texanna played her scales, Bill, enslaved,
        ate muscadines.
Texanna soon learned to play etudes.
           Waltzes and sonatas followed.

Bill had a banjo that he played alone,
        but when Texanna played piano
Bill would hide beneath her window
          swallowing muscadines like quarter notes.

Whatever afflicted Texanna afflicted Bill
        though Adeline blamed muscadines
for the slave's demise. Absalom and Adeline
        buried their daughter in view of the house
and built a fence to hold her there.

Three Women by the Pee Dee River

                    soft sprung
                              moss bank
    river named like a bird song
                              walk along
              boats along
                              boats along
    the bird song river
                              cargo boats
    boats of grain gain-
                              say boats of pain
              pain to see
                              boats of grain
    oaring down the bird song river
                              boatman's song
              oar to sea
                              or to see
              grain to sea
                              not me
        boats of grain
                              cargo boats
      boatman's song
                              boats along
    the birdsong river
                              rustle dress
              moss bank
                              soft spring
              not me

1861-1865

Letters by Fanny Little's brothers from battlefields in Virginia, Tennessee, and Georgia, Johnson Island's Prison, and from Mississippi. Letters to Fanny from her parents, Adeline and Absalom, and her cousin, Anne, all in Mississippi.

Miss Fanny Is Needed Back Home

As I write the stillness is broken
by the low moan of Aunt Adeline.
>> The cook can see through the kitchen window
>>>>>> I am troubled in the mind.
>> her young daughter in the clinch of an overseer's hand,
The distressing news reached us through one of
the neighbor boys that Calvin was badly
>>>> brown feet scarcely scraping the ground.
wounded in the late battle at
Manassas Junction. Aunt Adeline
>>>>>> I am troubled in the mind.
>> She has been pulled from her sick bed to the whipping tree.
is in great distress for Cally is her
idol and a more deserving one
>>>>>>> Ask my Lord what I should do.
>> Now the cook is shoving torn rags into her ears
never had. She says if possible come
to her for if Calvin dies from his wound
>>>> as she prepares a hamper for
>>>> Miss Fanny's journey of mercy.
she thinks it will derange
>>>>>> I am troubled in the mind
or kill her.

Free as a Bird
After Robert Hayden

Thorn-deep deep deep   deep
            down where the frog sounds
night sounds
            black on black   tangle-deep cannot find you
down to the berry-banked waters
            wadeaway
descent of night

Armstead ran away and went to the Yankees
as Sherman's army was returning through
here to Memphis and I think we have others
that will go yet if they remain long in
Memphis. A great many have gone from here.
They are dying by the hundreds with smallpox
and other diseases. They know it, but
still they go. They wish to know for themselves
what it is to be free as a bird.

Many thousand gone

But I can see your silhouettes descending still
            shadows by the hundreds wordlessly descending
heads bent as though in prayer, processing
            downward yet your shadows rise
into that lacerating
            sanctuary to which we all are bound.

One Hundred Hams and Sam's Two Sons

I heard that Calvin and Albert were both
wounded at the battle of Gettysburg.
Albert shot through both thighs but no bones
broken—was very cheerful and is at
the hospital in Richmond VA.
Calvin was wounded by the fragments of a
shell. I dread to hear the correct account
of that battle for alas! I know
many, many of our brave boys found a
death bed there while others received wounds, but
to languish and die.

Old Satan is a busy old man.
He rolls stones in my way.

Oh it is sad to see how many hearts
and homes have been made desolate by this
cruel war and then to have the villains
exalt with fiendish glee over our distress.
I pray that you may never lay eyes
on the Yankee tribe for they are everything
that is mean and ungodly They have paid
us two visits—stole everything they could
get their hands on. They took over one hundred
hams, (all we had) what little salt we had.
They took Peter and Shade (Sam's two sons) and

Jesus is my bosom friend.
He rolls them out of my way.

eleven heads of horses and mules robbed
the negroes of clothing and money.
Nelson left taking with him Polly's
Rachel and Emma and Armstead's Judy.
I expect the last ones will leave. I have

Oh come, go with me.
Oh come, go with me.

not a particle of confidence in
any of them, they are certainly the
most treacherous race of people that ever
existed. But I am willing to let
all that property go so my boys are spared.

I really do believe I'm a child of God.
Walking in heaven, I roam.

Shrapnel

                                     I am beginning to get

uneasy again

                      no letter from him

since the middle of May there

          have scarcely been two days in any week

                              when it did not rain

Tennessee River on a pontoon bridge,

               arrived here tired, hungry

                        and wet

the march

      & is still

              raining my camp

there was peace and prosperity; now

                      there is confusion and disorder

         consequent upon this wicked war

            that is being waged against us

               but I believe all will be right in the end

            a just God will not allow

                such wicked and unholy design to

          wrote me that the hole

where the ball entered was nearly healed up

               but that he had little use of his shoulder

         and that he was fearful he would ever

              our total loss for all six days in killed

       wounded and missing was

twenty three

          going into the fight with only

forty two

          not kept myself entirely unspotted from the world,

       which we are told by the Apostle James constitutes

one of the first elements   pure

      and undefiled Religion before God

you can well imagine how much we have to strive
with the old Adam   clinging to
     Petersburg by R.R.,

                       bivouacked for the night
in the suburbs of that city
                 the news we have from Miss.
   and particularly from Vicksburg
       is still agonizing in the extreme
that she has suffered so patiently and then to be denied
      the privilege of seeing me in her last moments
         is harrowing
but it is a soldier's fate to be far
     not permitted any fires we have nothing to protect us
        but flies
    until I had lived on beef and bread and not enough of that
          I did not know what home was worth
       I have an abiding faith
 that any all wise Providence will yet visit a righteous retribution
on the heads of the guilty parties
                    and that
   we will yet emerge from the darkness that surrounds us
in an open old field exposed to both sun and rain
without any tents except such as we can make of our blankets and coats
     is ended we may all again meet under the Parental roof
         and receive the blessings of our aged father
   who bears so nobly under the indignities that have been heaped
      Howell Co and them   we'll not and true
       is false to
        able feeling
          's Atlanta
   Myers

Columns

Doric columns have been placed like sentries,
      two on each side of what should have stayed
a plain white farm house.
      Classical columns on a gabled porch cannot stop
quartering squadrons, nor dysentery.
      Unemptied chamber pots overflow.
The smell of death swells in the Mississippi heat.
      Their boys will all make it home, saying:
Jonesboro, Gettysburg, Vicksburg, Manassas,
      Chickamauga, Lookout Mountain, Appomattox. Saying:
shrapnel, amputation, right lung, prison camp,
      but Adeline and Absalom are dying

                        and the moon will turn to blood
                        and the moon will turn to blood
                        and the moon will turn to blood
                        in that day...Oh my soul
            and the moon will turn to blood in that day

Epilogue: February 12, 1983

My grandmother's house is empty now
except for one abandoned set of curtains
limp as death behind a decaying casement.
My grandmother's house is empty now
so why should this picture seem to show
a stranger's face looking down at me
from a window on the second floor?

The last Little to live here had been dead
since the fall, and so had my father.
My friends, as a birthday gift,
brought me here to photograph
what was before now no more than recollections
passed on by my father, denied admission
longer than I had lived over the legacy of litigations
and estrangements common among people
who have forgotten to remember what to love.

We circled one time around the house,
stopped in the yard for pictures,
and drove on to lunch in Greensboro
leaving behind us dust, leafless trees on a white sky,
and the suggestion of a face none of us had noticed
staring out the window of a neglected house.

Notes on the Poems

This collection of poems is not by any means intended to accurately reflect the history of Little's Mills. The narratives are fictional and relationships between people as well as between the people and the land are not intended to be taken literally. For example, I have no reason to believe Billy Little actually lived on the land that became known as Little's Mills, but I have incorporated letters to Billy Little into the poetry, as though he did. More information about these poems, along with scanned letters, complete song lyrics, and where available, links to the music, can be found at www.maryannadunnpoetand.com.

Littles' Mills or Little's Mills? I have entitled the book Letters to *Littles'* Mills because numerous people, all surnamed Little, lived on the property. The community was actually known as *Little's* Mills, as though one man could have accomplished so much by himself. I do not know what Little's Mills milled, but my father once told me that grain was transported down the Little and Pee Dee Rivers, as referenced in "Three Women Standing by the Pee Dee River."

Cover Photo. The photograph on the cover is one of those taken in the final poem, "Epilogue." This house was built at Little's Mills after the war and was the home of Fanny Myers Little from 1879 until her death in 1924. It was the family home my father knew, and although not antebellum, to me it is more symbolic of the on-going legacy of slavery than the original house, which has been largely frozen in time. Pictures of the original house are available on the website.

"Exchange of Goods." A *cabess* was a unit of 2000 cowrie shells. During the American slave trade era, cowrie shells were a form of African currency. The *cabess* was named for a prominent family of African human traffickers. My resource for information about human trafficking during the American slave era was Hugh Thomas's *The Slave Trade: The Story of the North Atlantic Slave Trade: 1440-1870* (1999, Simon and Schuster).

"Aprons Are Very Fashionable." More commonly spelled "sack", a *saque* was a dress with a length of fabric attached in the back, near the top. I deliberately altered the spelling to the less standard form in order to avoid confusion with the cloth bag.

"A Wedding Gift." I am grateful for my poetic license, which I used in order to move Emmy from her family in Mississippi to North Carolina. Fanny Myers Little was already married and living at Littles' Mills when her family moved to Mississippi. Emmy is a fictional character and I have no reason to believe, or not believe, that Fanny was "given" any child as a wedding present.

"Miss Fanny is Needed Back Home." The story of a sick child being whipped by an overseer within hearing of her mother is a fictionalized version of a story I have heard about a cook at Jefferson's Monticello and her flu stricken son, beaten within sight of his mother for allegedly malingering. "Jean" was denim, just as it is today. Linsey-woolsey was a cheap, coarse material common in the colonial era but later worn mostly by enslaved people, especially children.

Never able to separate her concern for children's issues from her passion for writing, **Mary Anna Dunn** discovered long ago that she had to serve two masters. Mary Anna has worked in the field of education since 1985. She is the founder and director of The Enrichment Alliance of Virginia, an educational non-profit dedicated to enriching the out-of-school time of under-served children in and around the Charlottesville community. She is an active member of VSA Arts Charlottesville/Albemarle.

A native of North Carolina, Mary Anna has lived in the Virginia Blue Ridge since 1984. She holds a BA in Psychology from Guilford College, an MA in English Literature, Language, and Pedagogy from the University of Virginia, and an Ed.D. in Curriculum and Instruction from the University of Virginia.

Publications in which her work has appeared include *Inkwell, New Millennium Writings, Tar River Poetry,* and *Portside.* In *Letters to Littles' Mills*, Mary Anna weaves together spirituals and original poetry with letters to her ancestors as she tries to imagine the lives of the people her family enslaved.

Fifty percent of any profits Mary Anna should receive from this chapbook will be donated to non-profit organizations that improve the lives of people impacted by the legacy of slavery.

www.ingramcontent.com/pod-product-compliance
Lightning Source LLC
LaVergne TN
LVHW051612080426
835510LV00020B/3252